The Oxford Piano Method

Piano Time Sports

Book 2

T0056993

Fiona Macardle

MUSIC DEPARTMENT

OXFORD
UNIVERSITY PRESS

OXFORD
UNIVERSITY PRESS

Great Clarendon Street, Oxford OX2 6DP, England
198 Madison Avenue, New York, NY10016, USA

Oxford University Press is a department of the University of Oxford.
It furthers the University's aim of excellence in research, scholarship,
and education by publishing worldwide

Oxford is a registered trade mark of Oxford University Press
in the UK and in certain other countries

© Oxford University Press 2003

Fiona Macardle has asserted her right under the Copyright, Designs
and Patents Act, 1988, to be identified as composer of this work.

Database right Oxford University Press (maker)

First published 2003

All rights reserved. No part of this publication may be reproduced,
stored in a retrieval system, or transmitted, in any form or by any means,
without the prior permission in writing of Oxford University Press,
or as expressly permitted by law. Enquiries concerning reproduction
outside the scope of the above should be sent to the Music Copyright
Department, Oxford University Press, at the address above

Permission to perform the works in this anthology in public
(except in the course of divine worship) should normally be obtained
from the Performing Right Society Ltd. (PRS), 29/33 Berners Street,
London W1T 3AB, or its affiliated Societies in each country throughout
the world, unless the owner or the occupier of the premises
being used holds a licence from the Society

Permission to make a recording must be obtained in advance
from the Mechanical Copyright Protection Society Ltd. (MCPS),
Elgar House, 41 Streatham High Road, London SW16 1ER,
or its affiliated Societies in each country throughout the world

18

ISBN 0-19-372774-9

Music and text origination by
Barnes Music Engraving Ltd., East Sussex
Printed in Great Britain on acid-free paper by
Caligraving Ltd., Thetford, England.

With many thanks to my own teachers:
Josephine O'Carroll
Fintan O'Carroll
Eric de Courcy
Margaret Bowden

Piano Time Sports

If you're fighting fit after book 1, then it's time to turn the training up a gear! Athletes increase the level of their training over time to maintain and improve stamina, and practising technical exercises on the piano works in exactly the same way. If your hands get in the habit of having a thorough workout, you'll get your muscles in peak condition and develop your skills so that you'll be able to play the pieces you want. Your new fitness programme starts here!

There are 10 sessions, each focusing on a particular technical point. Each session contains:

- ***Warm ups:*** first, a very simple workout of a bar or two for repetition, so that you can concentrate on the technique rather than the notes. Try hands separately and together. Try them in different keys and in different octaves on the piano. Try playing them with different dynamics. 'Coach's tip' helps you get the best out of these. Second, a warm up, also based on the technique, for the piece on the opposite page.
- ***Midweek training:*** a short, simple piece practising the new technique.
- ***Fitness level:*** a more extended piece, also based on the technique, and designed to show off your new-found skill!

Contents

Session 1	*Broken chords*	*page* 4
Session 2	*Chromatics*	6
Session 3	*Travelling fingers*	8
Session 4	*Repeated (staccato) sixths*	10
Session 5	*Pedal*	12
Session 6	*Independence of hands*	14
Session 7	*Octaves*	16
Session 8	*Finger dexterity*	18
Session 9	*Preparation for turns*	20
Session 10	*Developing scales*	22

Session 1: *Broken chords*

Warm ups

Coach's tip: Try these with your eyes closed. Think about where your hands will go before you play.

1.

2.

Warm up for ***Mountain race***

1.

2.

3.

Midweek training: *Cross-country run*

Smoothly

mf

cresc.

f

dim.

p

Mountain race

Session 2: *Chromatics*

Warm ups

Coach's tip: Keep your hand shape neat when you play the chromatic scale.

Warm up for ***Scaling the cliffs***

Midweek training: *The climbing wall*

Scaling the cliffs

At a comfortable pace

Session 3: *Travelling fingers*

Warm ups

Coach's tip: Practise substituting the fingers slowly at first. Keep your hand relaxed.

Warm up for ***Learning to ride***

Midweek training: *Saddling up*

Learning to ride

Scherzando

mf *sfz*

f

sfz

rall. poco a poco

ff *dim.* *mp*

p **gallop away!** *f* *sfz*

Session 4: *Repeated (staccato) sixths*

Warm ups

Coach's tip: When you start this exercise, relax your hand between the chords. If you have very small hands, you may need a rest from time to time.

Warm up for ***Snookered***

Midweek training: *Cueball*

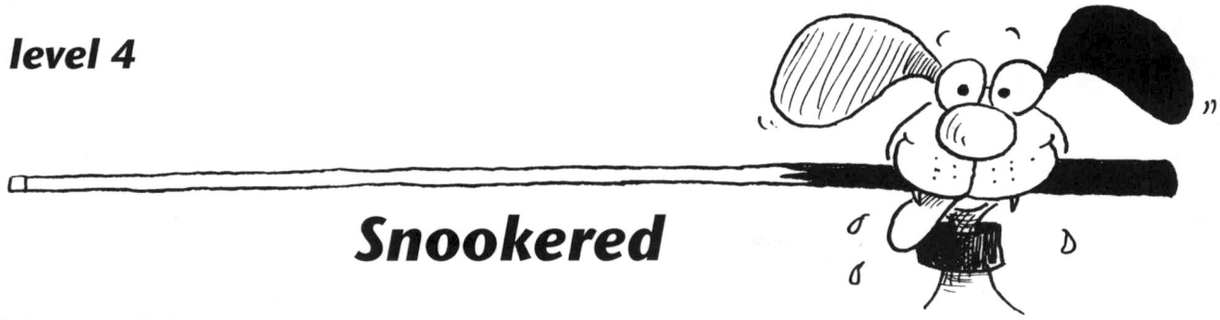

Snookered

With confidence

f *mp* *f*

mp *p*

mf *cresc.*

f *mf* *f*

p *dim.* *pp* *ppp*

Session 5: *Pedal*

Warm ups

Coach's tip: When you can do these chords slowly, lifting the pedal and reapplying it without interrupting the sound, then take the exercise at a slightly faster pace. Your foot should be in contact with the pedal at all times.

1. 2.

Ped. Ped.

3. 4.

Ped. Ped.

Warm up for ***Sailing home***

1.

5 5

Ped.

2.

3

Ped.

Midweek training: *Calm at sea*

Misterioso

pp

5 5 5

Ped.

5 3 4 2

dim.

5

Sailing home

Session 6: *Independence of hands*

Warm ups

Coach's tip: To begin with, practise each hand separately, then play both hands together—SLOWLY!

Warm up for ***The velodrome***

Midweek training: *Freewheeling*

The velodrome

With a sense of momentum

Session 7: *Octaves*

Warm ups

Coach's tip: After a while, try guessing the octave distance with your eyes closed.

Warm up for ***Pole-vaulting***

Midweek training: *The high jump*

Pole-vaulting

Session 8: *Finger dexterity*

Warm ups

Coach's tip: Lift your fingers like horses lift their knees. Keep your hand curled and your wrist not too high.

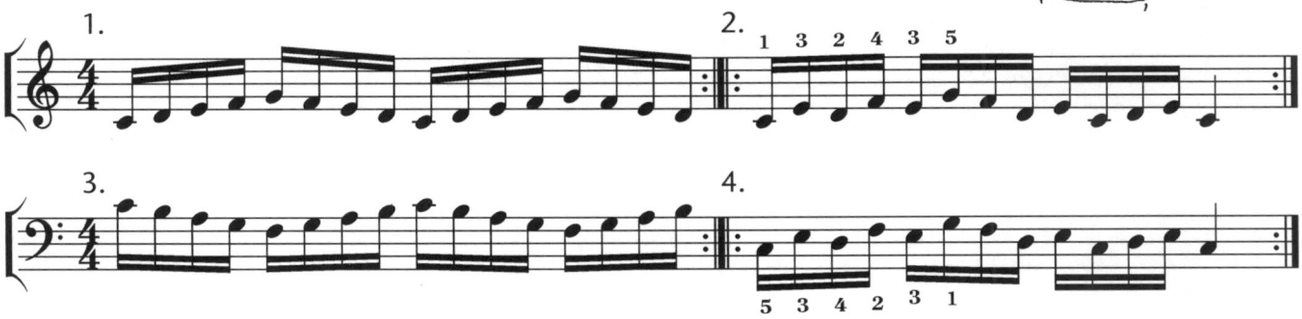

Warm up for ***The challenge***

Midweek training: *Pre-match pep talk*

With enthusiasm

The challenge

Forcefully

fff

sfz

meno f

mf

ff

fff

Session 9: *Preparation for turns*

Warm ups

Coach's tip: Keep your thumb well tucked under so that it is ready when needed.

Warm up for ***On the trapeze***

Midweek training: *Somersaults*

On the trapeze

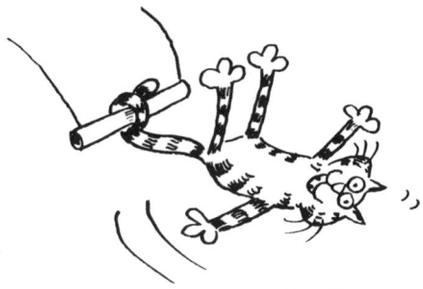

Evenly and at a comfortable speed

Session 10: *Developing scales*

Warm ups

Coach's tip: Think about where your scale is aiming for rather than about each individual note.

Warm up for ***Lap of honour***

Midweek training: *Out of the pits*

Lap of honour

Triumphantly

mp

cresc.

mf

mp

cresc.

f

1.

2.

Fine

f

mf

D.C. al Fine

PIANO TIME SPORTS

Certificate

This is to certify that

_____

has completed

Piano Time Sports

Book 2

_____ _____

TEACHER'S SIGNATURE DATE